Quiz: 138863

Level: 3

Points: 0.5

S0-ARK-828

Seven Oaks Elementary
Media Center

Virginia

BY HOLLY SAARI

Seven Oaks Elementary
Media Center

The Child's World

Published by The Child's World®
1980 Lookout Drive • Mankato, MN 56003-1705
800-599-READ • www.childsworld.com

ACKNOWLEDGMENTS
The Child's World®: Mary Berendes, Publishing Director
The Design Lab: Design and production
Red Line Editorial: Editorial direction

PHOTO CREDITS: Klaas Lingbeek-van Kranen/iStockphoto, cover, 1, 3; Matt Kania/Map Hero, Inc., 4, 5; David Coleman/iStockphoto, 7; iStockphoto, 9, 10, 17; Newton Page/iStockphoto, 11; Bryan Hemphill/Photolibrary, 13; North Wind Picture Archives/Photolibrary, 15; AP Images, 19; Caitlin Mirra/Shutterstock Images, 21; One Mile Up, 22; Quarter-dollar coin image from the United States Mint, 22

Copyright © 2011 by The Child's World®
All rights reserved. No part of this book may be reproduced or utilized in any form or by any means without written permission from the publisher.

LIBRARY OF CONGRESS CATALOGING-IN-PUBLICATION DATA
Saari, Holly.
  Virginia / by Holly Saari.
      p. cm.
  Includes bibliographical references and index.
  ISBN 978-1-60253-491-9 (library bound : alk. paper)
  1. Virginia—Juvenile literature. I. Title.

F226.3.S23 2010
975.5—dc22

                        2010019405

Printed in the United States of America in Mankato, Minnesota.
July 2010
F11538

30922061087   Virginia

On the cover:
Monticello was the home of Thomas Jefferson, the third president of the United States.

CONTENTS

Geography

Let's explore Virginia! Virginia is in the east-central United States. The Atlantic Ocean is to the east.

OHIO

PENNSYLVANIA

WEST
NORTH
EAST
SOUTH

MARYLAND

NEW
JERSEY

DELAWARE

WEST VIRGINIA

Front Royal •

Arlington •
Alexandria •

KENTUCKY

Allegheny
Mountains

Blue Ridge Mountains

• Charlottesville

Richmond
★

Roanoke •

Appomattox •

VIRGINIA

Williamsburg
•
Jamestown •
• Yorktown
• Newport News
Norfolk •
• Virginia Beach
Chesapeake •

TENNESSEE

Atlantic
Ocean

NORTH CAROLINA

SOUTH CAROLINA

5

Cities

Richmond is the capital of Virginia. Virginia Beach is the largest city in the state. Norfolk, Charlottesville, Arlington, Newport News, Williamsburg, Chesapeake, and Roanoke are other well-known cities.

Richmond was the capital of the Confederate States of America during the U.S. Civil War.

More than 190,000 people live in Richmond. ▶

Land

The Allegheny and Blue Ridge mountains are in western Virginia. The Shenandoah Valley is in the middle of these mountain ranges. The central part of the state is hilly. Coastal **plains** are in the eastern part of the state.

Wildflowers grow in the Blue Ridge Mountains. ▶

Plants and Animals

Forests cover more than 60 percent of Virginia. The state tree and the state flower are the dogwood. It is a tree that has flowers. Animals such as bears and deer live in the forests. The state bird is the cardinal. Male cardinals are bright red. Females are often brown and red.

Dogwood trees **bloom** in the spring. ▶

People and Work

About 7.8 million people live in Virginia. Most people live in large cities. Some people are government workers. Other people work in **tourism** or printing. Farming is also important in the state. Tobacco, chickens, and cattle are grown and raised here. Ships are built in cities near the ocean. Food, fabric, and paper products are also made in Virginia.

A tourism worker shows visitors Williamsburg's history. ▶

History

Native Americans have lived in the Virginia area for thousands of years. In 1607, people from Europe founded Jamestown. It was the first **permanent** settlement in America. Soon the land around Jamestown was called Virginia. England ruled the land. The **colonies** fought Britain during the **American Revolution**. They formed the United States. Virginia became the tenth state on June 25, 1788.

Jamestown settlers explored the area and built forts. ▶

Ways of Life

Many battles of the American Revolution and the Civil War happened in Virginia. These battles are important parts of the state's history. Some people act out battles of the Civil War.

Visitors to Virginia can see the beautiful mountains, beaches, and old homes.

People act out a famous Civil War battle that took place in the ▶ Shenandoah Valley in October 1864.

Famous People

Eight U.S. presidents were born in Virginia. These include George Washington, Thomas Jefferson, and James Madison. Booker T. Washington was born in the state. He opened an important school for black people in the late 1800s.

Booker T. Washington was born a slave in 1856. He was freed after the Civil War. ▶

Famous Places

Mount Vernon was George Washington's home. It is a **popular** place to visit. Thomas Jefferson's home, Monticello, is also in Virginia. Arlington National Cemetery is in the state. People who have served in the **armed forces** are buried here.

The Natural Bridge is another famous place to visit. It is a large rock bridge that is not man-made.

More than 4 million people visit Arlington National Cemetery each year. ▶

State Symbols

Seal

The goddess Virtus is on Virginia's state seal. She has beaten Tyranny, who is on the ground. Go to childsworld.com/links for a link to Virginia's state Web site, where you can get a firsthand look at the state seal.

Flag

A colored state seal is on the Virginia state flag. The flag was adopted in 1861.

Quarter

The Virginia state quarter shows ships that brought people from Europe to settle the Virginia area. The quarter was released in 2000.

Glossary

American Revolution (uh-MER-ih-kin rev-uh-LOO-shun): During the American Revolution, from 1775 to 1783, the 13 American colonies fought against Britain for their independence. Many battles of the American Revolution took place in Virginia.

armed forces (ARMD FOR-sez): Armed forces are a country's military. Members of the armed forces are buried in Arlington National Cemetery.

bloom (BLOOM): To bloom is to open up. Dogwood trees bloom in spring.

Civil War (SIV-il WOR): In the United States, the Civil War was a war fought between the Northern and the Southern states from 1861 to 1865. Many Civil War battles were fought in Virginia.

colonies (KOL-uh-neez): Colonies are areas of land that are newly settled and controlled by a government of another land. The American colonies fought against Britain to gain freedom.

Confederate States of America (kun-FED-ur-ut STAYTS UHV uh-MAYR-uh-kuh): The Confederate States of America was the group of 11 states that left the United States to form their own nation during the U.S. Civil War. Virginia was part of the Confederate States of America.

permanent (PUR-muh-nunt): Something permanent stays in place. Jamestown was the first permanent settlement in America.

plains (PLAYNZ): Plains are areas of flat land that do not have many trees. Virginia has plains.

popular (POP-yuh-lur): To be popular is to be enjoyed by many people. Mount Vernon is a popular place to visit in Virginia.

seal (SEEL): A seal is a symbol a state uses for government business. Virginia's state seal shows a goddess.

symbols (SIM-bulz): Symbols are pictures or things that stand for something else. The seal and the flag are Virginia's symbols.

tourism (TOOR-ih-zum): Tourism is visiting another place (such as a state or country) for fun or the jobs that help these visitors. Tourism is popular in Virginia.

Further Information

Books

Edwards, Pamela Duncan. *O is for Old Dominion: A Virginia Alphabet*. Chelsea, MI: Sleeping Bear Press, 2005.

Keller, Laurie. *The Scrambled States of America*. New York: Henry Holt, 2002.

Thornton, Brian. *The Everything Kids' States Book: Wind Your Way Across Our Great Nation*. Avon, MA: Adams Media, 2007.

Web Sites

Visit our Web site for links about Virginia: *childsworld.com/links*

Note to Parents, Teachers, and Librarians: We routinely verify our Web links to make sure they are safe and active sites. So encourage your readers to check them out!

Index

Seven Oaks Elementary
Media Center